BRITAIN
SINCE
1930

G000069950

Contents

The 1930s

Introduction   2

Growing up in the 1930s   4

Britain at work   6

Out of work in the 1930s   8

Transport and holidays   10

Entertainment in the 1930s   12

The 1940s

The Second World War   14

The Blitz   16

The home front   18

After the war   1945–50   20

The 1950s

Housing in the 1950s   22

Growing up in the 1950s   24

Entertainment in the 1950s   26

'You've never had it so good'   28

The 1960s

The swinging 60s   30

Growing up in the 1960s   32

Sport and leisure in the 1960s   34

Main events of the 1950s and 1960s   36

Emigration and immigration   38

The 1970s and 1980s

Changes in work and roles   40

Science and invention   42

The environment   44

Looking back   46

Index and Glossary   **48**

SENU
COALISLAND

Introduction

There are still many people in Britain who were alive in the 1930s. How many do you know? They have seen many changes over the last 60 or so years, but not all things have changed. As you read through this book compare lifestyles in the past – in the 1930s, 40s, 50s and 60s – with lifestyles today. What things have changed? What things have stayed the same?

Housing in the 1930s

The way people lived in the 1930s very much depended on how much money they had. Rich families lived in large houses and sometimes had several servants. Poor families often lived in old, terraced, back-to-back houses.

A lot of new houses were built in the 1930s. Many people lived in semi-detached houses, which they either bought or rented. Most new houses were built to a similar design. Upstairs they had three bedrooms, a toilet and a bathroom. Downstairs they had a living room, dining room and a kitchen. New houses also had their own garden.

By the 1930s many houses were getting electricity. Electric lights made a lot of difference to people's lives. New electrical equipment also made housework easier.

A house in the 1930s may have looked like this inside.

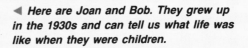

LOOKING AT EVIDENCE

◀ *Here are Joan and Bob. They grew up in the 1930s and can tell us what life was like when they were children.*

▼ *These are photographs of Joan and Bob when they were children. Ask your family if they have some old photographs.*

▶ *Many houses from the 1930s are still lived in today. Joan grew up in this house. It didn't have a bathroom. The only toilet was at the bottom of the yard.*

Growing up in the 1930s

Children started school at the age of five. Most left at the age of 14 and went straight to work. Many stayed at the same <u>elementary school</u> from the age of five to 14.

Most elementary schools were old. They had little space for PE or games. Children spent most of their time at school learning the three "R"s – Reading, wRiting and aRithmetic.

Some boys and girls took a scholarship exam when they were 11. If they passed they could go to a secondary or grammar school, where they could stay until they were 18.

> I liked school.
> I got one of the highest marks in Sheffield in the scholarship exam.
> My parents couldn't afford to send me to a grammar school. They couldn't afford to buy the books or the school uniform.

> I hated school.
> Teachers were very strict and often caned pupils.
> We rarely had games.
> I was glad to leave.

◀ *Elementary schools were very overcrowded. There were often more than 40 children in each class.*

Childhood illness

In the 1930s many children caught serious illnesses. Every year several thousand children died from infectious diseases, like diphtheria, measles and whooping cough.

I caught scarlet fever and diphtheria. I was very ill and was off school for over nine months.

▲ *Children swinging on a lamppost in the street.*

What did children play?

Popular 1930s toys included whips and tops, yo-yos, wooden hoops, Meccano, wooden scooters (often home-made), dolls and clockwork trains. Many children played indoor games like 'Snakes and Ladders', 'Ludo' and 'Monopoly'. Children in the 1930s often collected things, like stamps and cigarette cards.

There were not many cars on the roads so children played all kinds of street games, like hopscotch and marbles. Children often raced down the streets in go-carts or with hoops and sticks.

▶ *A sailor doll.*

◀ *A collection of 1930s cigarette cards.*

Britain at work

Most boys and girls started work at 14. Boys did a variety of jobs, depending on where they lived. In country areas boys often went to work on farms. Many farms still used horses to do much of the farm work, but these were gradually being replaced by tractors. As a result, there were fewer jobs on farms so many young people had to leave the country to work in the towns.

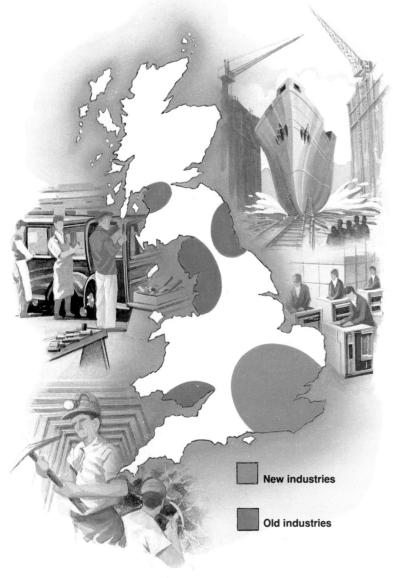

New industries

Old industries

▲ *Map of Britain showing areas dominated by old and new industries in the 1930s.*

Old industries

In the North of England, Wales and Scotland, boys often went into the same jobs as their fathers. They worked in coal mines, iron and steel foundries, textile mills and shipyards. There were fewer jobs, however, in these 'old' industries and many coal miners, iron and steel workers, textiles workers and shipbuilders were unemployed.

New industries

In the South and Midlands many people worked in the 'new' industries making cars, aircraft, chemicals and electrical goods. There were lots of office and banking jobs, and also jobs in the building industry.

Jobs for women

Girls had more choice of jobs than ever before, but it was still difficult for them to enter the professions, for example to be a doctor or lawyer. Most girls worked as waitresses, maids, shop assistants, typists, factory workers, teachers or nurses.

Most women earned less than men. They often had to give up work when they got married, as they were expected to spend their time working in the home and looking after the family.

In some professions, for example teaching, laws prevented women from working once they were married.

▶ *Nurses at work in the 1930s.*

◀ *Women working on a production line making radios in a factory in Manchester, 1935.*

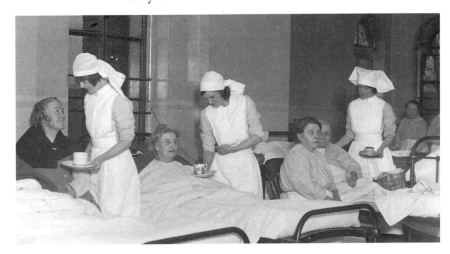

The working day

People worked long hours: ten hours a day was not uncommon. However, people in the 1930s worked fewer hours than people in the 1920s. By 1939 most workers were even given a week's paid holiday.

Here are some typical 1930s wages.

1933 WAGES (per week)

London bus driver £4.25
Farm worker £1.75
Female typist £2.50
Coal miner £3.00

1933 PRICES

Electric radio £15
Radiogram £28
Bicycle £4
Three-piece suite £10
Mars bar 1p
Tennis balls ....6p each

These wages do not sound much but things were much cheaper to buy than today. In fact, many goods came down in price in the 1930s. For those with a steady wage, falling prices meant a rising standard of living. For those in work, the 1930s were good times.

Out of work in the 1930s

In the early 1930s there was a decrease in world trade, which meant there was less demand for goods. Many factories had to close, and people lost their jobs. The depression was worldwide, and Britain suffered less than the USA or Germany. Even so, by 1932 some three million British people were unemployed.

Unemployment was heaviest in certain parts of Britain, especially those parts which had depended on 'old' industries – coal, iron and steel, shipbuilding and cotton.

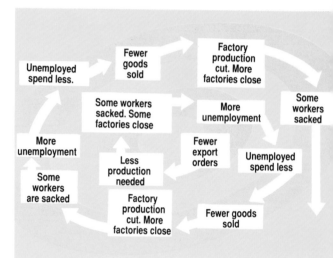

▲ This diagram shows how the depression grew in the 1930s.

▼ In 1936 200 men marched from Jarrow to London in an attempt to bring their unemployment to the Government's attention.

8

The dole and the means test

The unemployed received unemployment pay (dole) from the government. The government, however, was in trouble as it got less money from taxes because so many people were out of work. At the same time the government had to pay more dole money. The government tried to save money by cutting unemployment pay by 10%.

The government also introduced a means test. All men on the dole had to answer questions about their means (income). If they had some savings, or other members of their family earned some money, then their dole allowance was cut.

The Jarrow Crusade

One of the worst-hit places in Britain was Jarrow, a shipbuilding town on the River Tyne. There was no demand for ships, and soon about 75% of the men in Jarrow were without jobs. In 1936 some 200 unemployed men marched the 480 km from Jarrow to London. The Jarrow Crusade got a lot of publicity, but the government did little to help.

However, by the end of the 1930s the threat of war created many jobs in factories making guns, tanks and aircraft. New ships were ordered so there was plenty of work in Jarrow.

POINTS OF VIEW

Some people think the government should have done more to help the unemployed in the 1930s. Others think there was little the government could really do to help. What do you think?

Life on the dole

For the unemployed and their families life was hard. They had very little to spend on food, clothing, furniture or leisure.

◀ Breakfast: bread, margarine and tea.

▶ Queuing at the Labour Exchange.

◀ Receiving his dole money.

▶ Looking for cheaper food.

◀ Lunch: cheap meat stew or fish and potatoes, bread and tea.

▶ Looking for jobs advertised in the library.

◀ Wandering through the streets to pass time.

▶ Home for supper: bread, margarine and tea.

Transport and holidays

In 1930 only one million people owned a motor car. However, cars came down in price and by 1939 there were more than two million cars on Britain's roads. One family in ten had their own car.

People still travelled by steam train if they were making long journeys. Heavy goods were also transported by train. However by the end of the 1930s there were more lorries and vans.

▲ 1930s advertisement for a car. Not many people could afford to buy cars in the 1930s. This car cost £210.

▶ Milkman delivering milk and groceries in London in 1931.

> My dad was a tram driver. It wasn't a bad job but he couldn't afford to buy a motor car.

In towns the most common form of public transport was the electric tram. There were also trolley buses and ordinary buses. Horses and carts were still used and some people pushed hand carts carrying goods like fruit, milk and fish, from street to street, shouting out what they had to sell. Few people had fridges so housewives liked to buy fresh food whenever they could.

▲ *Bob on holiday in Blackpool with his mum and dad.*

▶ *Bank Holiday crowds on the beach at Margate.*

▼ *The* Queen Mary.

Seaside holidays

In the 1930s many people had a week's seaside holiday. Places like Blackpool, Scarborough and Brighton were very popular. People often went on the beach fully clothed!

We went on holiday to places like Yarmouth and Morecambe. We stayed in boarding houses. I didn't know anybody who went abroad for their holidays.

Aircraft were getting faster and safer, but few people could afford to travel by plane. Rich people who could afford to travel to America went by sea. The most famous passenger ships were the *Queen Mary* and *Queen Elizabeth*.

11

Entertainment in the 1930s

Many people in the 1930s had more money to spend on leisure. By 1939 most families had a radio or <u>wireless</u> set. The BBC controlled radio and there were only two choices of programme. Commercial radio stations were not allowed. Children often listened to *Children's Hour* at 5 p.m. Adults listened to dance bands, plays, concerts and comedy shows. Television started in 1936 but very few people could afford to buy a TV set. Here is a typical day's radio programme:

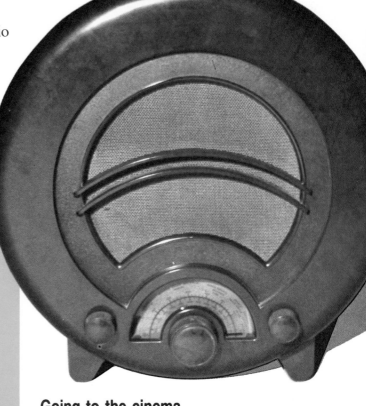

The Radio Times, 21 November 1935

a.m.

10.15	**Daily Service.**
10.30	**Time. Weather and Shipping.**
10.45	**Bath Pump Room Orchestra.**
11.45	**Organ Recital.**

p.m.

12.15	**Parker–Crook Trio.**
1.15	**City of Birmingham Orchestra.**
2.00	**Imperial Hotel Orchestra.**
3.00	**The Band of the Royal Marines.**
4.00	**The West Country Gazeteer.**
4.45	**BBC Northern Ireland Orchestra.**
5.15	**Childrens Hour: Meet Mickey Mouse.**
6.00	**Time. First News. Weather.**
6.30	**The Wallsend Shipyard Prize Band.**
7.55	**Anona Winn and her Winners.**
8.15	**The Royal Philharmonic Society's Concerts.**
10.15	**Time. News Summary. Weather.**
10.25	**The Cansal Club Orchestra.**
12.00	**Close Down.**

Going to the cinema

Many people went to the cinema. Some went two or three times a week. There were nearly 5,000 cinemas (or picture palaces) in Britain by 1939.

I usually went to the pictures twice a week. Most of the films were in black and white and were made at Hollywood in America.

The cinema was good value. You saw two full length films and a newsreel - all for 6d (2p)!

Music

Young people liked to listen and dance to swing bands. There were a lot of dance-halls. The foxtrot, rumba and waltz were all popular dances. Band leaders, like Henry Hall and Ambrose, were the pop stars of the day. Bing Crosby was a popular singer.

Some people owned a gramophone. This was like a record player but it had to be wound up by hand. Records only played for a few minutes and then the gramophone would start to slow down.

▲ *A gramophone.*

◀ *A 1935 wireless set.*

▶ *A picture palace in 1939.*

▼ *A collection of popular 1930s children's comics.*

Books and newspapers

Reading was a popular pastime. Paperback books were first published in the 1930s. Crime writers like Agatha Christie were very popular. Local libraries were well used.

Most adults bought newspapers. Children bought comics. Smaller children might read *Tiny Tots*. Older children bought *The Magnet* or the *Girl's Own Paper*. In the *Daily Express* there was a Rupert Bear cartoon strip which was very popular with children.

THE 1940s

The Second World War

In September 1939, Adolf Hitler, the leader of Germany, attacked Poland. Britain and France had promised to support Poland and so they declared war on Germany.

▲ **Winston Churchill.**

◄ **Adolf Hitler.**

▼ **The Battle of Britain**

◄ **Map showing Europe in 1939–40.**

■ Neutral countries

■ Britain stands alone

■ Occupied countries

■ Germany and countries allied with Germany

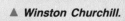 German invasions

Germany quickly defeated Poland and in 1940 Germany overran Denmark, Norway, the Netherlands, Belgium and France. British troops were cut off in France. Hundreds of small boats crossed the English Channel and rescued the British soldiers from Dunkirk. Hitler now controlled most of Europe.

Winston Churchill, the new British Prime Minister said, "We shall defend our island, whatever the cost may be . . . we shall never surrender." Britain prepared for a German invasion. Beaches and roads were guarded.

Thousands of people joined the Home Guard. The British navy controlled the seas. Hitler would not invade Britain unless the German Luftwaffe (air force) controlled the skies. From July to September 1940, the RAF fought a battle with the Luftwaffe. This is known as the Battle of Britain. The RAF did not let Hitler have control of the skies, and so Hitler decided not to invade Britain. Winston Churchill praised the RAF pilots. "Never," he said, "was so much owed by so many to so few."

By 1941 Britain was fighting Italy and Japan as well as Germany. But Britain did have the support of the British Empire and the help of Russia and the USA.

In 1942 British troops defeated the Germans and Italians at the battle of El Alamein in North Africa. "Before El Alamein we never had a victory," said Churchill. "After El Alamein, we never had a defeat."

In 1943 Britain invaded Italy, which was allied with Germany. On 6 June 1944, D-day (deliverance day) – British and American forces landed in Normandy in France.

▲ *Women worked long hours in factories making weapons for the British forces.*

Everybody in Britain was expected to help the war effort. All men between the ages of 18 and 41 could be <u>conscripted</u> into one of the armed forces, or to take part in special war work, for example, making aeroplanes. Some were employed as coal miners.

Many women volunteered for the women's armed services. They did a lot of essential jobs but were not expected to fight. Soon it was almost impossible for women under 40 to avoid war work. They did many jobs that men had done before the war. Some joined the Women's Land Army and worked on farms.

Children helped by collecting scrap iron which could be turned into weapons. Many knitted scarves and socks for servicemen.

The Blitz

At the start of the war everyone expected that the Germans would bomb British cities. Some thought they would use poison gas, so everyone was given a gas mask which was supposed to be carried at all times. However, the Germans didn't use poison gas and soon people stopped carrying gas masks.

Evacuation

In 1939 hundreds of thousands of children were evacuated from Britain's main towns. They went to country areas where there was less chance of being bombed. Most children were placed with strangers, and although some liked their new foster homes many were homesick. The Germans didn't bomb British cities in 1939, so many children returned home.

▲ *Damage in London following a V1 attack. Look for the Anderson air raid shelter and the Air Raid Wardens sorting through the bomb damage.*

▼ *Children being evacuated in 1940. They have name labels and they are carrying gas masks.*

Anderson shelters were built of corrugated iron and covered with earth. Inside there were bunk beds, food and candles.

Morrison shelters could be used as tables. One of the wire sides could be lifted from the shelter, so people could crawl inside.

Air raids

Air Raid Wardens were appointed. One of their jobs was to make sure that all lights were hidden after dark so that enemy planes could not find their targets. There were no street lights and all windows were covered up. People were not even supposed to light a match. Cars had to cover their headlights. It was dangerous to go out at night!

In the autumn of 1940, a year after the war had started, the Germans finally bombed Britain. The German bombing is known as the Blitz. Most of Britain's main towns were bombed, and London was bombed by German planes night after night.

There were various types of air raid shelters. Anderson shelters, put up in gardens, could hold six people. Morrison shelters could be used as tables inside houses. Many Londoners spent the night sheltering in Underground railway stations. It was noisy and crowded but at least it was safe.

In June 1941 Hitler attacked Russia. German air raids became less frequent. British and American planes now bombed German cities. Germany suffered far more damage than Britain.

V1s and V2s

In 1944 the Germans came up with a new threat – flying bombs and rockets. The V1 flying bombs, or doodlebugs, were small planes with no pilot. The V2 rockets travelled faster than sound, so no one heard them until the bomb exploded.

Over 60,000 British people were killed by German bombs. More than half of these people died in London. But German bombers and rockets did not force Britain to surrender.

POINTS OF VIEW

German cities suffered far more from bombing than British cities. Some people think that Britain and America were right to bomb German cities. Others think the strategy was wrong. What do you think?

The home front

During the Second World War German U–boats (submarines) sank many ships bringing supplies to Britain. This meant that there was a shortage of everything, especially food. Everyone was encouraged to 'Dig for Victory' and grow food. People dug up their lawns and planted potatoes, and some kept chickens.

Rationing

To make sure that food was fairly shared out, everyone had a ration book. Shopkeepers tore coupons out of these books and gave food in return. Butter, jam, sugar and sweets were all rationed. Other types of food, like meat and fruit, were very scarce. At least there were plenty of vegetables and people were encouraged to eat carrots and potatoes.

Most British factories made goods needed for the war, so many other things were rationed, including clothes. Women were encouraged to 'make do and mend'. Dusters, sheets and tablecloths were all used to make new clothes or to mend old garments.

▲ *Wartime ration books and clothing coupon books.*

There was no petrol for family cars. Coal was rationed. There was a paper shortage, and, as a result, newspapers became smaller. Children collected waste paper, jam jars and rags. Everything was useful to help the war effort.

The government did its best to keep up people's spirits. Many news stories were banned if it was felt they might upset people or damage the war effort.

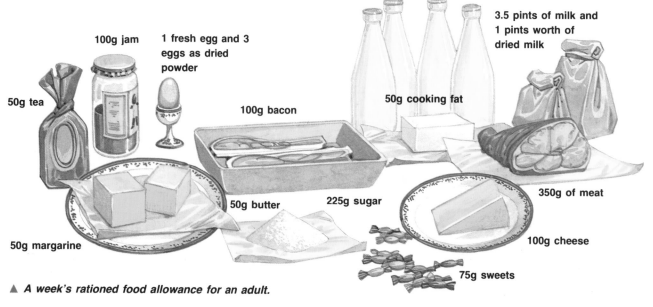

100g jam

1 fresh egg and 3 eggs as dried powder

3.5 pints of milk and 1 pints worth of dried milk

50g tea

100g bacon

50g cooking fat

50g butter

225g sugar

350g of meat

50g margarine

100g cheese

75g sweets

▲ *A week's rationed food allowance for an adult.*

▲ *VE Day celebrations in May 1945.*

▼ *An atom bomb explosion.*

Making the best of things

People learnt to carry on and make the best of
things. They still listened to the wireless,
danced and went to the cinema. Many children
found the war exciting. Schools often suffered
bomb damage and were closed. There was a
good team spirit. Most people felt they were
working together to beat the enemy.

The end of the war

In 1945 the Second World War ended.
Germany was invaded by British, American
and Russian troops. Adolf Hitler committed
suicide and Germany surrendered. May 8th,
1945, was VE (Victory in Europe) Day. There
was great rejoicing in Britain. There were street
parties, bonfires and singing. In August 1945

the USA dropped atom bombs on two
Japanese cities – Hiroshima and Nagasaki.
Thousands of people died and Japan surrendered.
The Second World War was over. Nearly
400,000 British people died during the war.

After the war – 1945–50

▲ *Queuing for rationed goods.*

Most people looked forward to a better life in 1945, but things did not immediately improve. The war had been very expensive, and there was terrible bomb damage. During the war Britain had had to borrow millions of pounds to pay for vital food and materials, and now owed huge amounts of money to the USA. She had lost many of her markets for her export products and most British firms had not enough money to replace old machinery.

Rationing continues

In the late 1940s there was a shortage of almost everything. Food (even bread and potatoes), paper, coal, petrol and clothing were still rationed. People were asked to use only 7cm of water when they had a bath, as this saved fuel. The winter of 1947–48 was very cold. Power stations ran out of coal, and electricity had to be shut off several times a day.

I married Bob in December 1945. He left the army a few months later. We had no house and little chance of getting one. For two years we had to live with my parents.

By 1948 rations were lower than they had been during the war. Queuing was a part of life.

There was also a shortage of houses. Five million had been destroyed or damaged during the war and few new houses had been built. Prefabricated houses or 'prefabs' were made in factories. They could be built quickly and they were cheap to buy.

1943	1944	1944
Ministry of Town and Country Planning	**Education Act**	**Family allowances**
		1946
		National Insurance Act (allowances for the old, sick and unemployed)
Squalor	**Ignorance**	
1948	**1946-1970**	
National Health Service	**Full employment**	
		Want
Disease	**Idleness**	

▲ *This diagram shows the main acts that were introduced by the British government.*

▶ *A waiting room in a National Health Service surgery, 1949.*

▼ *A family outside their prefabricated house, in 1945.*

The new Labour Government

In the 1945 General Election more people voted for the Labour Party than for Winston Churchill's Conservative Party. The new Labour Government wanted to change things.

In 1942 a civil servant called William Beveridge had written a report about poverty. He said there were five giant evils: disease, want, ignorance, idleness and squalor. Beveridge thought it was the government's job to do something about these evils and to help people 'from the cradle to the grave'. The Labour Government agreed and tried to build a Welfare State.

Many people thought the most important act was the introduction of the National Health Service. Everyone now had a right to free medical treatment, hospital care, dental care and 'National Health' spectacles. The National Health Service was not really free. It had to be paid for through taxation and workers paying insurance. But 'free' health care did take a lot of worry away from some people.

21

Housing in the 1950s

◄ *An aerial view of part of Harlow, a new town.*

▼ *This tower block in London was built in 1956.*

In the 1950s new housing estates were built all over Britain, usually on the edge of towns. Whole new towns like Corby, Harlow and Peterlee were also built. The structures of these new towns were planned by architects. They had modern road systems and new shopping centres, and the houses were built away from the factories. These towns took up large areas of the countryside.

At the end of the 1950s some town councils began to build high-rise blocks of tower flats. These took up less of the countryside, but many people did not like living in them.

LOOKING AT EVIDENCE

▶ *Bob and Joan have three children. Alan was born in 1948; Anne was born in 1953 and David was born in 1959. Alan and Anne grew up in the 1950s and can remember what it was like. (David can't!)*

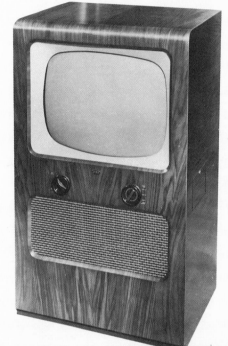

Many objects from the 1950s – records, toys, comics and electrical goods – can still be found today.

◀ *A 1950s television set.*

▶ *This is the cover of a popular Bill Haley record that was released in 1958.*

I made and lit the fire each morning. It was a messy job.

◀ *Here is a typical 1950s living-room. In what ways is it different from a 1930s room? In what ways is it different from a typical living-room today?*

Growing up in the 1950s

After the Second World War a lot of babies were born. By the 1950s the 'baby boom' children were ready to go to school. Many schools had been damaged during the war. A lot of new schools had to be built. Many of these are still used today.

Primary schools

In all primary schools, each child was given a free one-third of a pint of milk each day. Children were often put into different classes. Those who were thought to be clever went into the A class. Other children went into the B or C classes.

▲ Here is a primary school class in the 1950s. What strikes you most about the class and the classroom?

◀ Children drinking their school milk at a primary school in 1952.

I went to a new primary school. It had a lot of windows and was surrounded by grass. It was easy to play football, cricket and rounders.

I was a milk monitor. I had to give out milk and straws at playtime. We saved milk tops to buy guide dogs for the blind.

POINTS OF VIEW

Some people thought the 11+ exam was a good way of deciding which schools children should go to. Others thought the exam was unfair. What do you think?

Grammar and secondary modern schools

In the last year of junior school most children took the "Eleven Plus" (11+) exam. Those who passed this exam went to grammar school. Those who failed went to secondary modern school. Far more children failed than passed. Grammar and secondary modern schools were supposed to be equal but people thought grammar schools were better as the children who passed the 11+ exam went there.

Grammar school pupils studied for exams which they took when they were 16 and 18. Many went on to university. Others went to teacher training colleges. Some got jobs in professions like banking or the civil service.

Secondary modern schools offered more practical subjects like art, craft, gardening, needlework and cookery. Many secondary modern pupils left school with no qualifications and went straight into a job at 15. Others became apprentices or learned new skills at evening classes.

National Service

Almost all young men had to spend two years in the armed forces when they reached the age of 18. This was called National Service. The aim was to keep the navy, army and air force strong in case there was another war.

Entertainment in the 1950s

The coronation of Elizabeth II at Westminster Abbey in 1953 was televised, and watched by many people in their homes.

▼ **Andy Pandy** *was one of the most popular children's television programmes in the 1950s.*

Television

In the early 1950s radio was still the main form of home entertainment. BBC now broadcast on three radio channels.

At the start of the 1950s few people had televisions. They were expensive to buy. There was only one channel (BBC) and this used to stop broadcasting between 6 and 7 p.m. so that parents could get their children to bed! There were many gaps – or 'interludes' – and television closed down at 10.30 p.m. Television screens were much smaller than they are today.

After the Coronation of Elizabeth II, more people bought televisions. There was no colour television but screens grew in size. In 1956 ITV began broadcasting. ITV had more popular programmes than BBC. They had quiz shows like *Take Your Pick* and *Double Your Money* and serials like *Emergency Ward Ten*.

Television made a tremendous change to family life. By 1959 many families watched television for more than four hours a day, and children spent less time playing outside. Television had an effect on the cinema too: in 1953 most people went to the cinema at least once a week; by 1959 fewer people went and many cinemas were forced to close down. Many were turned into bingo halls. Theatres and music hall variety shows also suffered as more people bought televisions.

I thought ITV was much better than BBC. ITV had children's programmes like *Ivanhoe*, *Robin Hood* and *The Buccaneers*.

My parents bought a TV set in 1952. In 1953 the whole family crowded round their television to watch the coronation of Queen Elizabeth II.

◀ *A family at home watching a modern television in the late 1950s.*

Sport

Large crowds still went to football and cricket matches. Some of the major sporting events were now shown on television. Many people remember watching Stanley Matthews in the Cup Final in 1953, Roger Bannister running the first mile in under 4 minutes in 1954, and Jim Laker taking a record 19 wickets in a test match against Australia in 1956.

▲ *Roger Bannister's record-breaking run in May 1954.*

'You've never had it so good'

▲ Harold Macmillan.

▼ Advertisement for a washing machine in 1957.

Lucky Me!

"I ENJOY A LIFETIME OF WORKLESS WASHDAYS—
I can complete the whole family wash in two minutes.
All I have to do is put in the clothes, set the dials and
add the soap. My BENDIX does all the hard work and
is so economical, I save time, money and hot water".

Yes, the BENDIX soaks and washes a full
9-lb. load and rinses three times in fresh,
clean water each time, using in all only
twelve gallons of hot water—other wash-
ers use as much water for the wash period
alone. Finally, the machine spins the
clothes damp dry ready for the line or
dryer.

BENDIX is simple to install;
it has a flat porcelain enamel
table top and fits snugly into
a space of only 2 ft. square

BENDIX *automatically* THE BEST!

SOAKS · WASHES · RINSES THREE TIMES
DAMP DRIES · DRAINS AND SWITCHES ITSELF OFF

BENDIX HOME APPLIANCES LTD. (DEPT. 1), ALBION WORKS, KINGSBURY ROAD, BIRMINGHAM, 24

In 1959 the Conservative Prime Minister Harold Macmillan told the British people, "You've never had it so good". In many ways he was right. The 1950s was a prosperous time for most people.

Machines began to do a lot of jobs previously done by people, so people worked fewer hours. A five-day week and an eight-hour day became common and most people received a fortnight's paid holiday each year. Wages went up and there were plenty of jobs.

In 1954 rationing finally came to an end. People were now able to buy sweets, clothes and petrol without ration books. Many large new supermarkets opened up.

> I didn't go out to work. Like most married women, I stayed at home. My job was to look after the family. New electric gadgets meant that housework became easier.

All kinds of new goods – washing machines, televisions, fridges and telephones were now available. These goods were now mass-produced so they were cheaper to buy.

Most families could afford to go on holidays to British seaside resorts. Children enjoyed going to holiday camps where there was plenty of entertainment.

People were healthier, and ate more and better food. Most children were vaccinated against diseases like measles, whooping cough and scarlet fever.

Teenagers

Young people or 'teenagers' also had more money to spend. They had their own fashions. Fashions were always changing.

Teddy boys dressed in drainpipe trousers, long coats and boot-string ties. They wore winkle-picker shoes. Their hair was greased back with Brylcreem. Those who were in fashion were 'with it' or 'cool'. Those who didn't fit in were 'squares'.

▲ When rationing finally came to an end in 1954, teenagers became aware of fashion and spent a lot of money on new clothes. Most girls wore dresses with fitted tops and full skirts but some wore trousers.

1 Elvis Presley.
2 Cliff Richard.
3 Buddy Holly and The Crickets.
4 Teddy boys listening to a juke box in a coffee bar.

Teenagers also had their own music – rock 'n' roll. By the end of the 1950s American rock 'n' roll singers like Elvis Presley, Little Richard and Buddy Holly were very popular. There were also British pop singers, like Tommy Steele, Lonnie Donegan and Cliff Richard.

Some teenagers liked to go to coffee bars which served foaming espresso coffee. They could listen to the latest records on the juke box and show off their clothes.

The swinging 60s

Until the 1960s the leading rock singers were American. The arrival of The Beatles in 1962–63 made British pop music popular throughout the world. 'Beatlemania' swept through Britain, Europe and America and the 'Fab Four' – John Lennon, Paul McCartney, George Harrison and Ringo Starr – were mobbed wherever they went.

Some pop groups represented the rebellious side of youth. The Rolling Stones shocked many adults. The Who smashed up guitars and drums on stage.

▲ The Beatles in concert, 1964.

◀ The Who.

▶ Carnaby Street in London was one of the fashion centres of the world in the 1960s.

Fashion

The 1960s saw a revolution in the way young people dressed. New materials like synthetic fibres and plastic were used. There was a great fashion boom and many small shops – or boutiques – sold imaginative clothes. The most 'trendy' boutiques were in Carnaby Street and the King's Road in London. London became the fashion centre of the world.

▲ *Most girls wanted to look young and slim, like Twiggy, the top model.*

Fashion trends changed very quickly. Skirts became shorter and shorter until some mini-skirts were only 30 cm long. This shocked some older people. Girls now wore tights rather than stockings.

Changes in men's fashion were even more startling. Men began to wear colourful clothes and to grow their hair longer. Some adults thought you couldn't tell the difference between men and women.

Mods, rockers and hippies

Teenagers in the 1960s did not all dress alike or think the same. There were different groups who had their own style of dress, hair, favourite music and types of behaviour.

Some people were mods. They liked to spend money on stylish clothes. They travelled around on scooters covered with badges, lamps and pennants. They wore khaki parkas. They liked pop groups such as The Who and The Small Faces.

Rockers dressed in black leather and rode large motorbikes. They greased their hair and liked rock 'n' roll music. On bank holidays, thousands of mods and rockers went to seaside resorts. Sometimes they fought pitched battles.

Later there were people called hippies. They wore very brightly coloured clothes and spoke of love and peace.

Growing up in the 1960s

◄ *During the 1960s there were many student demonstrations.*

► *This comprehensive school was built in the late 1960s, during the Labour Government.*

▼ *Many universities and colleges were built and extended in the 1960s. This building at the University of East Anglia was built in 1962.*

Many young people in the 1960s wanted to be different from their parents. They had different points of view to their parents, and thought that adults should take notice of their opinions.

Some young people were optimistic. They thought they could change the world and make it a better place.

University students protested about lots of things – the way their universities were run, the Vietnam War, apartheid in South Africa, and the Nuclear Bomb. 1968 saw student unrest in the USA, France, West Germany and Britain. There were more students than ever before because more universities and colleges had been built.

The 1960s was an exciting time for many teenagers. People spoke of a youth revolution. It affected everything from music and clothes to politics and religion. Teenagers often followed the lead of their pop heroes like The Beatles. The Beatles became more 'way out' towards the end of the 1960s.

Changes in education

In the early 1960s many people felt that the 11+ exam, which was used to decide which children went to grammar schools and which went to secondary modern schools, was unfair. The Labour Government which came into power in 1964 supported the idea of comprehensive schools where children of all abilities could be taught together. By 1969 many pupils went to comprehensive schools.

Primary schools no longer had to push children towards the 11+ exam so new forms of teaching were tried out. Instead of learning poems by heart and reciting multiplication tables, there was more project work and more practical learning.

Many teenagers still left school at 15. There were plenty of jobs. Few people were unemployed.

LOOKING AT EVIDENCE

1960s pop songs and record covers can give us a lot of information about the 1960s. This is the record cover for one of The Beatles hit records.

Come mothers and fathers
   throughout the land,
And don't criticise what you
   can't understand.
Your sons and your daughters
   are beyond your command,
Your old world is rapidly ageing.
Please get out of the new one if
   you can't lend your hand,
For the times they are a-changing.

▲ *Here are the words of a popular Bob Dylan song. What do they tell you about the 1960s?*

Sport and leisure in the 1960s

▲ Transistor radios were popular in the 1960s.

▼ Radio Caroline was transmitted to Britain from this ship in the North Sea.

▲ Popular Radio 1 disc jockeys in the 1960s were Jimmy Saville (top) and Tony Blackburn (bottom).

Most people in the 1960s had more money to spend and more leisure time than ever before. By 1969 nine out of every ten houses had TVs. BBC 2 started in 1964 and colour TV in 1967. Most people had record players or tape recorders. They bought lots of records. Many also had small, portable transistor radios.

In 1967 BBC started Radio 1. This was for young people and played non-stop pop music. Radio 1 disc jockeys became famous. Before this, Pirate radio stations set up transmitting pop music from ships on the North Sea. The government however declared these 'pirate' stations illegal.

Sport

Sports, like football and cricket, remained popular. Many British children idolized football heroes, like Bobby Charlton or George Best. The best English teams were Tottenham, Manchester United and Leeds United. The Scottish team Celtic was the first British side to win the European Cup.

In 1968 the Wimbledon tennis tournament allowed professional tennis players to play for the first time. Ann Jones won the Women's Singles in 1969 by beating Billie-Jean King.

New sports centres opened, where people could swim and play squash or badminton. More people played golf and tennis. Ten-pin bowling was a craze for a while.

> I loved football. The best moment in the 1960s was when England won the World Cup in 1966 by beating West Germany at Wembley.

Holidays, cars and food

People had more money to spend on holidays. Many families bought caravans. Jet aircraft made air travel faster and cheaper, and package holidays, especially to Spain, became popular.

More people owned cars. The most popular car in the 1960s was the Mini. New motorways and by-passes were built so it was quicker to travel to places. It became more and more difficult to park in town centres even though new car parks were built and parking meters were introduced.

People often ate out, and Chinese restaurants became popular. Fast-food chains sprang up.

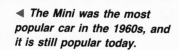

◄ *The Mini was the most popular car in the 1960s, and it is still popular today.*

Main events of the 1950s and 1960s

1950s

<table>
<tr><td>

BRITAIN

</td><td>

THE WORLD

</td></tr>
</table>

50

1950 Start of the Korean War. United Nations forces (mainly American but including some British) went to fight for South Korea against North Korea and communist China.

1951 Winston Churchill became Prime Minister again.

51

1951 The Festival of Britain was held in London to celebrate post-war progress.

52

1953 Mount Everest was climbed by Edmund Hillary and Sherpa Tensing.

1953 Queen Elizabeth II's coronation.

53

1953 End of the Korean War.

1954 Roger Bannister became the first man to run a mile in under four minutes.

54

1955 Winston Churchill resigned as Prime Minister.

1955 Ruth Ellis was the last woman to be hanged in Britain.

1955 Rock 'n' roll arrived in Britain.

55

1956 The Suez Crisis. Britain and France sent troops to Egypt to control the Suez Canal. America gave no support and the British and French troops had to withdraw.

56

1956 Elvis Presley's first record, *Heartbreak Hotel*, was released.

1956 The world's first large scale nuclear power station was opened at Calder Hill in Cumberland.

1956 Hungarian uprising against Communist rule. The uprising was crushed by Russia.

1957 Britain tested its own hydrogen bomb.

57

1957 France, Belgium, West Germany, Luxemburg, the Netherlands and Italy set up the Common Market.

1957 Russia launched *Sputnik*, the first satellite to orbit the earth.

1958 Manchester United lost seven players in the Munich air crash.

58

1959 The M1 opened.

1959 The Mini car was first launched.

59

1959 The American rock 'n' roll star Buddy Holly was killed in an air crash.

1960s

BRITAIN	THE WORLD

60   1960   John Kennedy was elected American President.

61   1961   The Russian, Yuri Gagarin, was the first man in space.

1961   The Berlin Wall was built, separating East and West Berlin.

1962   The Beatles had their first hit record - *Love me do.*

62   1962   The Cuban missile crisis nearly led to nuclear war between the USA and Russia.

1963   The Great Train Robbery. An armed gang stole £2,500,000 from a mail train.

63   1963   President Kennedy was assassinated in Dallas, Texas.

1964   Harold Wilson became Prime Minister.

64

65   1965   Large numbers of American troops were sent to fight in the Vietnam War.

1965   Winston Churchill died.

1966   Aberfan disaster. A landslide moved a vast coal tip down a hill and onto a school, 116 children and 23 adults died.

66

1966   England won the World Cup.

67   1967   Dr Christian Barnard carried out the world's first heart transplant in South Africa.

1967   The Six Day War. Israel fought against Egypt, Syria and Jordan.

68   1968   Murder of Martin Luther King, the American civil rights leader.

69   1969   Apollo II landed on the moon. Neil Armstrong and Buzz Aldrin were the first men to walk on the moon.

Emigration and immigration

In the 1930s Britain ruled a great Empire. After the Second World War, British power declined. Most countries within the Empire wanted to rule themselves. In 1947, India and Pakistan gained independence. By the end of the 1960s most other countries within the British Empire had also gained independence. Although they were no longer ruled by Britain, most still remained part of the Commonwealth and accepted Queen Elizabeth II as Head of State.

Over the last two centuries many people have emigrated from Britain to settle in parts of the British Empire. Popular destinations have been Australia, Canada and New Zealand.

Map of the British Empire in 1890.

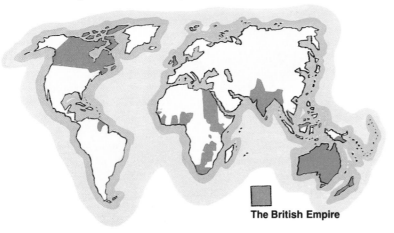

The British Empire

Map of the Commonwealth today.

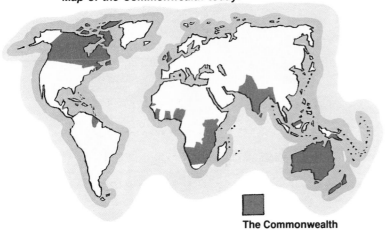

The Commonwealth

In the 1950s and 1960s about one million people from the West Indies, India and Pakistan came to settle in Britain. These countries had been part of the British Empire. Most of the immigrants came to Britain because they believed they could make a better life here. They were encouraged to come because there were many jobs that needed filling.

In the 1970s many Asians fled to Britain from Uganda, an African country. The Ugandan government forced them to leave. They came to Britain because Uganda had once been part of the British Empire and the Asian Ugandans still had British passports. In the 1980s many people came to Britain from Bangladesh and West Africa.

Multicultural Britain

Britain is now a multicultural society. The population in most towns includes people of many different races, colour and religion. The immigrants brought new ideas, music and foods to Britain.

In 1973 Britain joined most of the other West European countries in the Common Market (or EC). Common Market citizens are able to work in any of its countries.

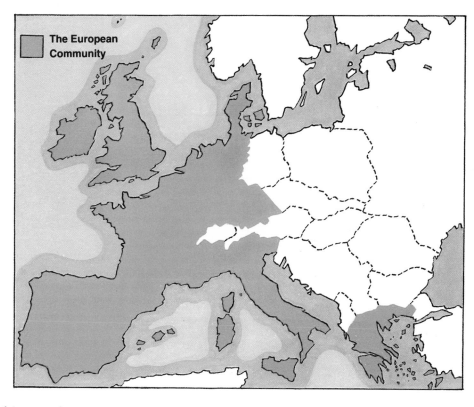

The European Community

▲ *Immigrants arriving at Gatwick airport in 1968.*

▶ *Map of the European Community.*

The new immigrants often settled in certain parts of Britain. Many West Indians settled in Brixton in London or in Birmingham. Many Pakistanis settled in Bradford and in 'old' cotton towns in Lancashire. Black and Asian immigrants often met racial discrimination and abuse. Many found it hard to get well-paid jobs. Some people refused to sell or rent their houses to immigrants.

RACE RELATIONS ACT
In 1968 a Race Relations Act was passed. This said that it was illegal to discriminate against anyone on grounds of race or colour.

Changes in work and roles

Working conditions have changed considerably over the last 20 years. In many factories much work is now done automatically by machines. Workplaces are more pleasant. However, fewer people are needed to do jobs.

Strikes

In the 1970s and early 1980s there were many strikes. Trade union leaders tried to protect jobs and get higher wages for workers. This was partly because of higher prices. But higher wages led to even higher prices. The result was inflation. Prices kept rising but money was worth less. Goods costing £1 in 1969 were costing nearly £3.50 by 1979. Strikes and inflation did not help the British economy.

▲ A modern car production line. Robots have now taken the jobs of many workers.

At the start and end of the 1980s there was high unemployment. British industry faced competition from overseas, especially Japan. There were fewer jobs in manufacturing industries, but many people found work in service industries, such as banking.

The winter of 1978-79 was dreadful. Everyone seemed to be on strike - dustmen, hospital workers, grave-diggers. Politicians called it the winter of discontent.

▲ Miners striking in 1985.

▲ *Margaret Thatcher was the British Prime Minister from 1979 to 1990.*

◄ *Women demonstrating for equality.*

The changing role of women

Until the 1960s women usually stayed at home and looked after the family. However, in the 1970s and 1980s more women took full-time jobs and were able to pursue their careers.

Many women were given poorly paid jobs. They had little chance of promotion. Some did the same work as men but were paid less. This was unfair, and women began to fight for equality. People called it 'Women's Lib', which was short for liberation.

Women proved they could do many of the jobs that only men had done in the past. In 1979 Margaret Thatcher became Britain's first female Prime Minister.

Women's roles have changed. Many women now go to college or university and get a good education and better jobs. Men and women now often share household tasks, such as housework and looking after children.

In the 1970s miners and power workers went on strike. Electricity was cut off. We had to use candles at night!

EQUAL PAY ACT

In 1970 the government passed the Equal Pay Act. Employers now had to pay equal wages to men and women doing the same job. The Sex Discrimination Act of 1975 made it illegal to discriminate against women in education, jobs or housing.

Science and invention

In the 1970s and 1980s there were great scientific advances. There were breakthroughs in medicine. Doctors carried out heart and lung transplants. New technology helped doctors to perform surgery and to recognise and understand illnesses. New drugs were discovered. People could now live longer than ever before.

Farmers introduced intensive farming methods to increase food production; hens were packed into battery cages, and powerful chemicals were used on the land.

New technology meant that Britain was able to develop her gas and oil reserves in the North Sea.

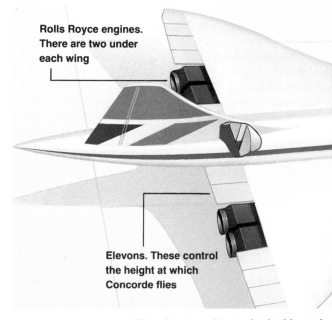

Rolls Royce engines. There are two under each wing

Elevons. These control the height at which Concorde flies

▲ *This diagram shows the inside and the outside of Concorde. Concorde became the world's fastest passenger aeroplane, flying on average 1,350 m p h.*

◄ *Large machinery enables farmers to harvest crops quickly and cheaply.*

▼ *Oil rig in the North Sea.*

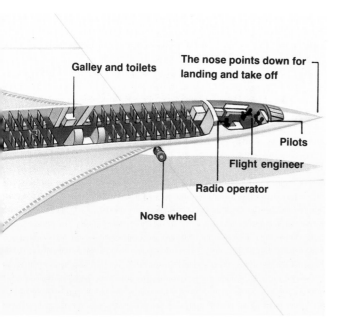

Galley and toilets

The nose points down for landing and take off

Pilots

Flight engineer

Radio operator

Nose wheel

Computers

Perhaps the greatest development in the 1970s and 1980s was in the field of computers. Thanks to the invention of the silicon microchip, computers became smaller and more powerful. By the early 1980s schools, hospitals and businesses all had computers. Many families also bought computers. Computer games became popular. Computers were used in more and more areas. These included petrol stations, cash dispenser machines, supermarket checkouts and in libraries. Computers could now do work once done by people, and this resulted in fewer jobs.

People talked of the 'Computer Age' which had started to revolutionise life both at home, at school and at work.

Transport and communications

Planes could now fly very fast. Concorde became the world's first supersonic passenger airliner. New motorways were built and cars became faster, safer and more reliable. New high-speed trains could travel at over 125 m p h (200 km p h). Britain and France began construction of the Channel Tunnel.

Satellites were sent into space. Television pictures could now be beamed live from most parts of the world in seconds.

By 1990 some people had compact disc (CD) players. Many families had video recorders, and some had video cameras. Satellite dishes, enabling people to get extra television channels, were introduced.

Pictures cannot be transmitted around the earth, as the earth's surface is curved. So they are transmitted to a satellite in space, and then the pictures are beamed down to the receiver's satellite dish on earth.

◀ *A microchip.*

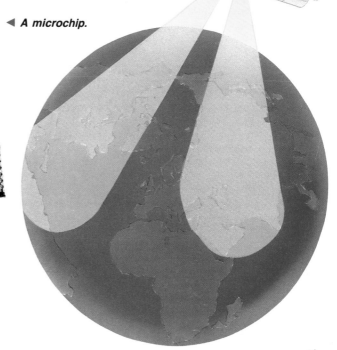

The environment

Over the last 50 years people have become more aware of the environment and more worried about pollution. Following the 1956 Clean Air Act, factory chimneys that sent out smoke into the atmosphere disappeared from the landscape. Instead, big power stations provided electricity for factories, schools, hospitals and homes. Unfortunately, coal power stations give off gases which cause acid rain.

In 1956 the government passed the Clean Air Act. This forced people in towns to burn only smokeless fuel. This did a lot to keep the air cleaner.

▲ *Before the Clean Air Act, cities in Britain were so polluted, that the air was smoky. This was called smog. People in the cities wore masks so they did not breathe the polluted air.*

Power

Scientists hoped that nuclear power might provide much of Britain's power. Calder Hill, the world's first nuclear power station, was opened in 1956. But some people were worried about nuclear power. A disastrous explosion at the Chernobyl nuclear power station in Russia in 1986 showed the dangers of nuclear power.

Britain was increasingly dependent on oil and gas. These supplies might one day run out. People hoped that wind, sun or sea might provide the power of the future without polluting the atmosphere.

▲ *The wrecked* Torrey Canyon.

▲ *There are many ways in which we can protect our environment.*

▼ *The nuclear power station at Bradwell, in Essex.*

Pollution

By 1970 some of Britain's rivers were so badly polluted that in many stretches there were no fish. There was also concern about pollution of the seas. In 1967 a huge oil tanker, the *Torrey Canyon*, was wrecked off the coast of Cornwall. Giant oil slicks formed on the surface of the sea. Thousands of sea birds died. Crude oil was washed ashore onto many of Britain's most beautiful beaches.

Car pollution became a major problem. More people used their own cars rather than public transport, and this caused traffic jams. Scientists were worried about the gases from car exhausts. In the 1980s lead-free petrol became widely used to prevent dangerous lead vapours polluting the atmosphere.

Britain's population continued to grow, and more roads and houses had to be built. There seemed a possibility that Britain would become one large town and that there would be no countryside left.

A Green Party was formed in the 1970s. The main political parties also became more concerned about environmental issues. Some efforts were made to reduce pollution. These included: cleaning up stretches of rivers; recycling rubbish; encouraging motorists to use lead-free petrol; and making sure that beaches are not polluted with sewage.

Looking back

Life in Britain has changed in many ways over the last 60 or so years. The diagram shows some of the main changes.

Some things have remained the same:

- Many people, like Bob and Joan, who were alive in the 1930s are still alive in the 1990s.

- Many people in the 1990s live in houses that were built or lived in during the 1930s.

- Many leisure activities and forms of entertainment are similar.

- Many of the things which are part of daily life in the 1990s (cars, telephones, fridges, etc) were around in the 1930s. It was just that few people could afford to buy them.

- There are still many people out of work.

1930s

Britain ruled a great empire.

Most people in Britain were white.

There were no televisions.

There were no computers.

Few people had cars.

Most children left school at 14.

Few women went out to work.

Few people had flown in an aeroplane.

Horses did a lot of farm work.

There were many small shops.

Few people had fridges or telephones.

Many men worked a 50-55 hour week.

People were lucky if they had a holiday abroad.

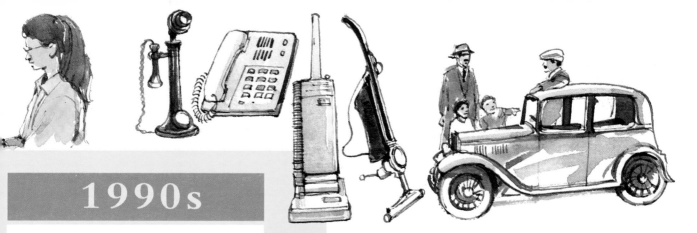

1990s

Britain no longer rules an empire.

Britain is now a multicultural society.

Most people have televisions and videos.

Computers play a big part in everyones lives.

Most people have cars.

Many pupils stay on at school or college until 18 - and beyond.

Many women have jobs.

Many people have been up in an aeroplane.

Most farms have modern machinery.

There are many large supermarkets.

Most people have fridges and telephones.

Most people work less than 40 hours each week.

Many people now have foreign holidays.

Bob and Joan were your age in the 1930s. They have seen many changes over the last 60 years. In many ways life has improved. But in some ways life has got worse. I wonder what changes you will see over the next 60 years?

There is more crime now than there used to be. Nowadays, many marriages end in divorce. They didn't in the 1930s.

Life today is better than it was in 1930. People are better fed and healthier. There are lots more things to do.

POINTS OF VIEW

Some people think that there has been tremendous progress over the last 60 or so years. But others are not so sure. Talk to your grandparents, and see what they think.

Glossary

These words are underlined in this book.

Acid Rain
Rain that contains chemicals which can destroy trees and vegetation.

Atom bomb
A bomb with a tremendous explosive capacity. The explosion results from the splitting of the atom.

Commonwealth
Most countries that were once members of the British Empire now belong to the Commonwealth. They recognize the British monarch as head of the Commonwealth.

Conscripted
During the war the government forced all people of a certain age to join the armed forces or to help the country in other ways.

Depression
A time of economic gloom during which many people are usually unemployed.

Discrimination
When people make distinctions between people, often because of their race, colour, sex or religion, and treat them differently and unfairly as a result.

Dole
Money paid by the government to people who are out of work.

Elementary schools
A school attended by children aged 5–14 during the 1930s and early 1940s.

Evacuation
During the Second World War, the government encouraged parents who lived in towns and cities to send their children to stay with families in safer country areas.

Inflation
An increase in prices and a fall in the value of money.

Multicultural
A society that has many different peoples, religions and cultures is known as a multicultural society.

Pirate radio station
Commercial radio stations (radio stations that make money by advertising) were not allowed to broadcast in Britain in the 1960s. Some pirate stations transmitted pop music into Britain from ships in the North Sea. The most famous pirate radio station was Radio Caroline.

Ration(ing)
This was introduced by the government during the Second World War. Food and other things in short supply were rationed. This meant that people could only buy a limited amount to ensure that the scarce goods were shared out equally and fairly.

Terraced houses
A row of houses that are joined together, and are of the same type.

Welfare State
The idea that the government should help everybody in society, especially those who are least able to help themselves, such as the old, young, ill, unemployed, etc.

Wireless
The 1930s and 1940s name for radio.

Women's liberation
A movement to give women more freedom and more equality with men.